Freshwater Giants

Hippopotamus, River Dolphins, and Manatees

Phyllis J. Perry

Franklin Watts
A Division of Grolier Publishing
New York • London • Hong Kong • Sydney
Danbury, Connecticut

For Julia, whose element is the water

Note to readers: Definitions for words in **bold** can be found in the Glossary at the back of this book.

Photographs ©: Animals Animals: 47 (Bruce Davidson), 12, 13 (Stefan Meyers); BBC Natural History Unit: 8 (Brian Lightfoot); ENP Images: 32 (Andy Caufield), cover (Brandon D. Cole), 10 (Michael Durham), 3 bottom, 20, 21, 46 (Gerry Ellis), 4 (Konrad Wothe); Innerspace Visions: 6, 7 (Mike Johnson); Marine Mammal Images: 49 (Thomas Henningsen), 30 (Mauricio Prieto), 9 (J. G. M. Thewissen); Peter Arnold Inc.: 40 (Fred Bavendam), 29 (Mark Carwardine/Still Pictures), 36, 37 (Luiz C. Marigo), 25 (Norbert Wu); Photo Researchers: 3 top, 34, 41, 42, 50 (Douglas Faulkner), 16 (Alan Root/Okapia/NAS), 28 (Varin Visage/Jacana); Phyllis J. Perry: 64; South American Pictures: 22 (Tony Morrison); Visuals Unlimited: 14 (Walt Anderson), 44 (Michael DeMocker), 17 (Gil Lopez-Espina), 15 (Glenn Oliver).

Maps created by Michael DiGiorgio

Visit Franklin Watts on the Internet at:
http://publishing.grolier.com

Library of Congress Cataloging-in-Publication Data

Phyllis J. Perry.
    Freshwater giants: hippopotamus, river dolphins, and manatees / by Phyllis J. Perry.
        p.   cm.— (Watts Library)
    Includes bibliographical references and index.
    Summary: Examines the physical characteristics, behavior, and habitats of three of the world's largest freshwater mammals: the hippopotamus, river dolphin, and manatee, and discusses some of the factors that threaten their survival.
    ISBN 0-531-11681-6 (lib. bdg.)   0-531-16424-1 (pbk.)
    1. Mammals—Juvenile literature. [1. Hippopotamus. 2. Manatees. 3. River dolphins.] I. Title. II. Series.
QL706.2.P47   1999
599.176—dc21
                                         98-25123
                                           CIP
                                         AC

Contents

Elephants are huge, but they don't even come close to being the largest animal in the world.

Chapter One

The Biggest Animals in the World

What's the biggest animal in the world? If someone asked you this question, what would you say? The elephant? The rhinoceros? These are both good guesses, but neither answer is correct.

Elephants are the largest living *land* animals. An Asian elephant may be up to 11 feet (3.4 meters) tall and weigh as much as 12,000 pounds (5,400 kilograms). African elephants are even larger. Even

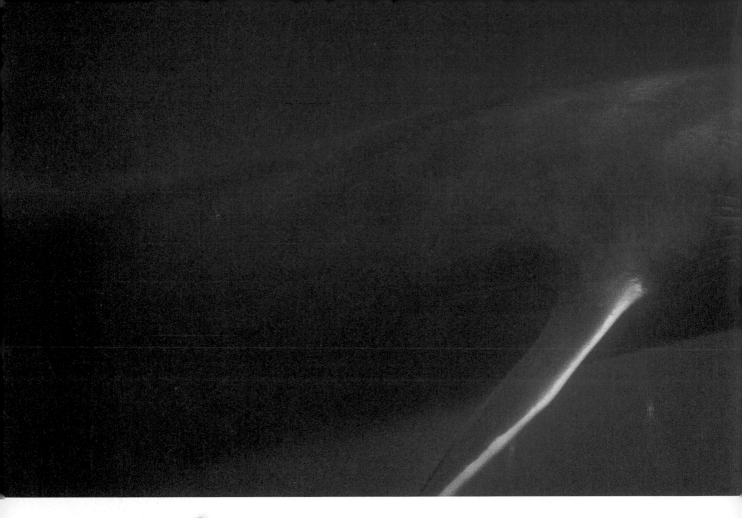

baby elephants are huge. At birth, an African elephant is about 3 feet (1 m) tall and weighs about 200 pounds (91 kg).

Rhinoceroses are gigantic, too. The Indian rhino may be 14 feet (4.3 m) long, weigh 8,000 pounds (3,600 kg), and stand about 6 feet (1.8 m) high at the shoulders. Elephants and rhinos are big, but neither comes close to being the largest animal in the world. The largest and most powerful animal on our planet is the blue whale. You may be surprised to learn that the blue whale is the largest animal to ever live on Earth. It is bigger than even the largest dinosaur.

When a blue whale is born in the spring, it is about 23 feet (7 m) long. By the end of its first summer, the whale is about 60 feet (18 m) long. An adult blue whale may be more than 100 feet (30 m) in length and weigh up to 284,000 pounds (128, 800 kg).

Like elephants and rhinos, whales are **mammals**. Even though they live in the ocean, whales have lungs and must come to the surface to breathe air. Like other mammals, whales are **warm-blooded**—they maintain a constant body temperature of 92° Fahrenheit (33° Celsius).

The majestic blue whale is the largest animal on Earth.

The Ancestors of Whales Lived on Land

Scientists believe that life on Earth began in the ocean about 3.9 billion years ago. Since 80 percent of the world's surface is covered by water, it is not surprising that a large number of amazing animals developed there.

About 440 million years ago, some ocean animals left the water and found ways to survive on land. Over time, a wide variety of warm-blooded land animals **evolved**. You might find it hard to imagine how ocean animals could develop into suc-

Warm-Blooded Versus Cold-Blooded

Most ocean animals—fish, jellyfish, clams, lobsters, sea stars, and others—are cold-blooded. Their body temperature matches the temperature of their environment. Many land animals are cold-blooded, too. Frogs, turtles, snakes, and snails breathe more slowly when the air temperature is cold. Their heartbeat is slower, too. As a result, these animals can't move very quickly. Have you ever seen a snake lying on a dark rock on a sunny morning? It was warming up so that it could move fast enough to catch its breakfast.

Warm-blooded animals—such as birds, mice, humans, and whales—regulate their body temperature. As long as you are healthy, your body temperature stays at about 98.6°F (37°C). Because your body temperature does not change with the air temperature, you can stay active all the time.

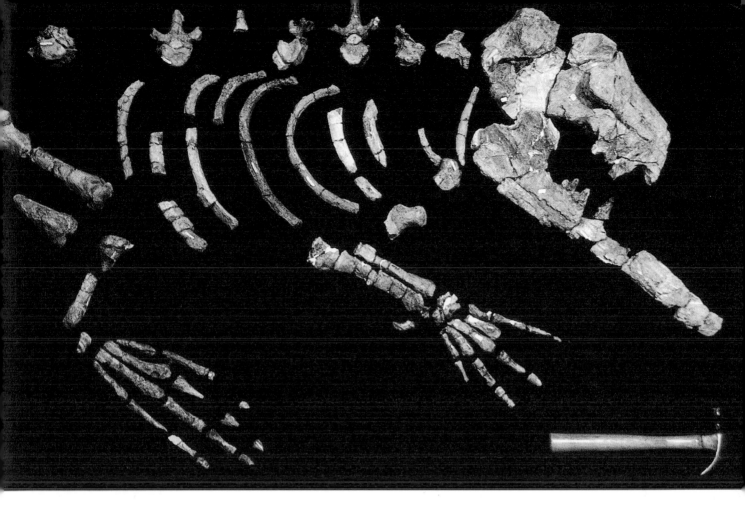

cessful land animals. Even more astonishingly, some of these land animals returned to the water about 45 million years ago.

By examining fossilized skeletons, scientists have discovered that the ancestors of whales once lived on land. Over time, those animals adapted to life in the ocean. For instance, their back legs disappeared and their front feet developed into flippers. If you compare the skeleton of a whale to a human skeleton, you will see that a whale's forelimbs have the same bone structure as our arms.

Ambulocetus, *a very early whale, was about the size of an adult sea lion. Its skeleton indicates that it could move about easily on land and in the water.*

The Freshwater Giants

While some early mammals adapted to life in the salty oceans, others developed body structures that allowed them to live in freshwater environments. This was no easy task. In many ways, living in freshwater is more difficult than living in the ocean. The environment of the ocean does not change very much, but freshwater environments change all the time. They heat up in summer and cool down in winter. When a river floods, fast-moving waters may carry animals downstream. If a drought occurs, a lake may dry up and the animals in it may die. If humans build a dam across a river, the flow of water—

Dams have an effect on the creatures that live in or near the water.

or even the course of the river—may change. Freshwater environments are also more sensitive to pollution.

In spite of all these challenges, many kinds of animals spend their entire lives in rivers, streams, lakes, and ponds. Most freshwater mammals, such as the beaver, the muskrat, and the otter, are small. But a few, such as the hippopotamus, the river dolphin, and the manatee, are much larger. These freshwater giants are the subject of this book.

Hippos spend most of their day in the water. This impressive group of hippos enjoys the waters of the Mara River in Tanzania, Africa.

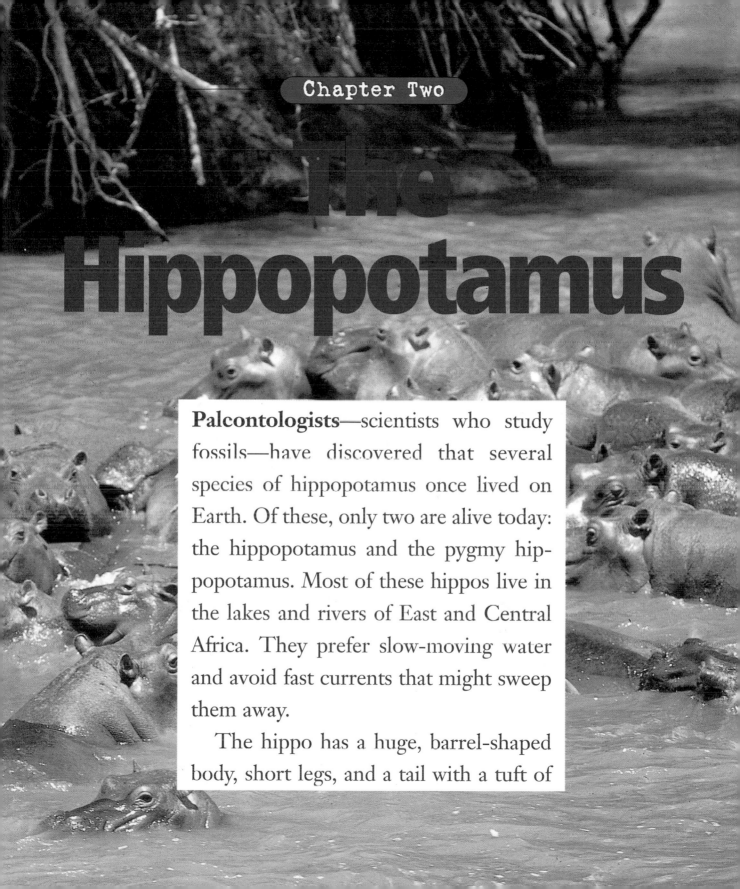

Chapter Two

The Hippopotamus

Paleontologists—scientists who study fossils—have discovered that several species of hippopotamus once lived on Earth. Of these, only two are alive today: the hippopotamus and the pygmy hippopotamus. Most of these hippos live in the lakes and rivers of East and Central Africa. They prefer slow-moving water and avoid fast currents that might sweep them away.

The hippo has a huge, barrel-shaped body, short legs, and a tail with a tuft of

The barrel-shaped body of this male hippo is scarred from past battles with other males.

hair at the tip. The average hippo is 12 to 14 feet (3.7 to 4.3 m) long and about 5 feet (1.5 m) tall at the shoulders. It's hairless skin is about 2 inches (5 cm) thick. When a hippo comes onto land, it loses water rapidly through its skin, and if it spends too much time out of water, it can **dehydrate**. The hide of a full-grown male hippo usually has many scars from fights with other male hippos.

A hippo has a huge head and an enormous mouth. Its jaws can open up to 4 feet (1.2 m) wide. The lower canine teeth of a hippo are razor sharp and up to 8 inches (20 cm) long. A hippo's eyes, ears, and nostrils are located on top of its head, so even when it is mostly underwater, it can still see, hear, and smell.

The skin on a hippo's back usually is grayish-brown to blue-black, while its belly is pink, but when a hippo sunbathes on the mudflats, it may change color. If a hippo gets too hot, **glands** in its skin produce a red liquid. This liquid seems to work like suntan oil, protecting the hippo's skin against sunburn. It may also contain chemicals that protect the hippo's skin from infection. The red liquid spreads over the animal's skin and dries like the glaze on a piece of pottery.

This hippo enjoys sunbathing on the mudflats. If it gets too hot, glands in its skin will produce a red liquid that may help protect the hippo from sunburn.

Hippos Are Pretty Speedy

Hippos usually move slowly in the water, but when they feel threatened, they can move with surprising speed. They can run up to 30 miles (48 kilometers) per hour for short distances.

A Hippo's Life

Most of the time, hippos get along well. An adult hippo spends most of the day resting in a water hole with 10 to 15 other hippos. Sometimes, as many as 150 hippos share the same water hole or stretch of river. While hippos are in the water, they either float on top or fill their lungs with air and sink to the bottom. Most hippos can stay underwater for up to 5 minutes before coming up for a breath of air.

Hippos leave the water at dusk and come onto land. In spite of their great size, they have no trouble climbing up the riverbank. Most of the time, they walk along well-worn trails. At the edge of these trails, male hippos leave piles of dung to mark their **territory**.

Hippos can spend up to 5 minutes at a time underwater.

During the coolness of night, hippos graze on grass and other plants. It may be hard to see hippos eating, but they're easy to find because they make a lot of noise when they eat. A hippopotamus eats about 88 pounds (40 kg) of grass each night. As the sun rises, the hippos return to the water, walking single file down the path they have made.

A male hippo, or bull, defends his territory and lives there with females and their young. Female hippos are called cows, and their babies are called calves. If one male enters another's territory, the bull who lives on that patch of land will try to frighten off the intruder. Hippos often turn their backs on each other, produce dung, and use their tails to scatter their droppings. One hippo may charge the other, and if one of the hippos does not leave, there may be a fierce battle. Two bulls may fight for up to 2 hours.

These male hippos are fighting a fierce battle in Kruger National Park, South Africa.

If a male hippo rushes into a part of the river next to land claimed by another male, the hippos will grunt, charge at each other, blow water out of their nostrils, and toss mouthfuls of water into the air. Then they use their sharp canine teeth

17

to cut and slash each other until one of the males retreats in defeat.

Hippos have a life span of about 40 to 50 years. A male hippo is considered a mature adult at about 7 years old. A full-grown male hippo may weigh up to 7,055 pounds (3,200 kg). The slightly smaller females usually weigh about 3,000 pounds (1,360 kg). The female is ready for mating when she is about 9 years old. Hippos usually mate in the water during the dry

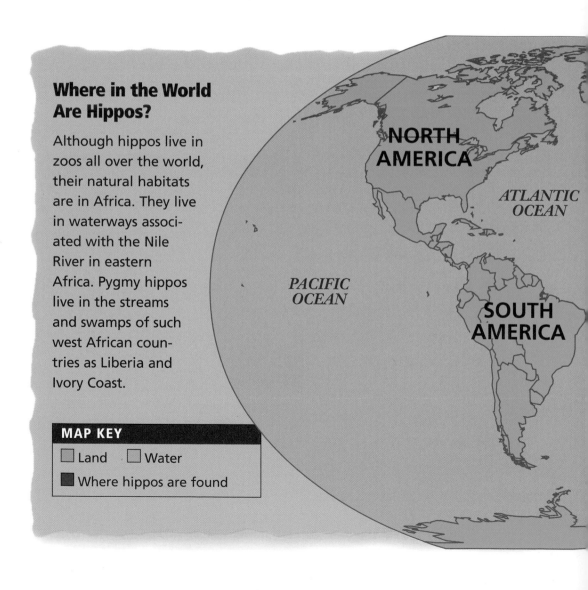

Where in the World Are Hippos?

Although hippos live in zoos all over the world, their natural habitats are in Africa. They live in waterways associated with the Nile River in eastern Africa. Pygmy hippos live in the streams and swamps of such west African countries as Liberia and Ivory Coast.

MAP KEY
☐ Land ☐ Water
■ Where hippos are found

NORTH AMERICA

ATLANTIC OCEAN

PACIFIC OCEAN

SOUTH AMERICA

season. This is when the population of hippos is usually most concentrated because water is scarce.

Young Hippos

Female hippos are pregnant for about 8 months. Baby hippos are born during the rainy season when food is easiest to find. Before giving birth, the female hippo leaves the group and goes off on her own. Calves are usually born underwater,

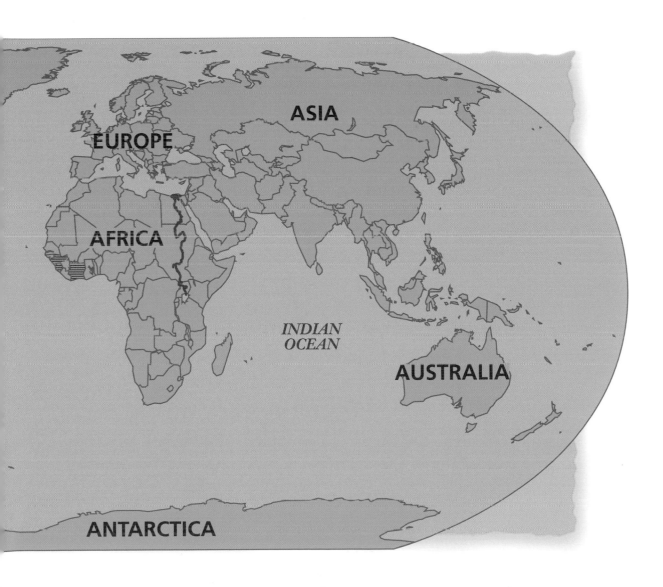

This young hippo calf trots along beside its mother, safe from its many enemies.

although they may also be born on land. Most of the time a female has just one calf, but twins are born about 1 percent of the time. Newborn hippos weigh about 93 pounds (42 kg).

If a baby hippo is born in the water, it swims to the surface immediately and takes a gulp of air. Then the calf nuzzles its mother, and begins to drink her milk. Calves can nurse on land or underwater. Often a newborn hippo rides on its mother's back when she is floating or swimming on the surface. About

2 weeks after the baby hippo is born, the mother and calf rejoin the herd.

Baby hippos face many dangers. About 45 percent of all hippos are killed during their first year of life. Their major enemies are lions, leopards, and hyenas. Occasionally, a baby hippo is captured by a hungry crocodile.

How Hippos Fit In

The hippopotamus plays a critical role in African river ecology. Hippo dung provides the **nutrients** that many water plants need to grow. The plants are then eaten by fish and birds, and these animals are eaten by crocodiles and other **predators**.

Hippos' habits may also cause problems. If they eat too much grass in one area, the land may be **eroded**—washed away by the wind or heavy rains. And eroded land cannot produce new grass for the hippos or other animals to eat.

The Samiria River, a tributary of the Amazon River, is home to many river dolphins.

Chapter Three

The River Dolphins

Imagine floating along the murky Samiria River in Peru on a wooden raft. At night you would hear chirping insects, croaking frogs, and the whistles and shrieks of strange birds and reptiles. You might even hear a bamboo rat crowing like a rooster. And, if you are lucky, you might also hear the huffing, snorting, and blowing of river dolphins.

Even if a dolphin came quite close, you probably wouldn't be able to catch a glimpse of it in the beam of your flashlight. But, in the moonlight, you might notice ripples in the water where the dolphin came up for air.

If you did see the dolphin, you would be amazed. The river dolphins that live in this area, the botos, are pink giants with whiskered snouts.

The Dolphin Family

The dolphin is closely related to the whale and the porpoise. All these creatures—dolphins, whales, and porpoises—live in water and look like fish, but they are not even closely related to fish. They are mammals, just like mice, elephants, dogs, cats, and humans.

There are about forty kinds of dolphins living on Earth today. Most of these dolphins live in the ocean, but a few have adapted to life in freshwater environments in tropical areas of the world. Many of these river dolphins have exotic sounding names—boto, susu, bhulan, baiji, and tucuxi.

Because they have long snouts, river dolphins resemble bottlenose dolphins that live in the ocean. Unlike ocean dolphins, river dolphins have flexible necks, so they can move their heads from side to side. River dolphins do not live in large **schools**. Instead, they live alone, in pairs, or in small groups.

Ocean dolphins often leap out of the water, so it isn't too hard to see what they look like, but river dolphins hardly ever jump. They only surface when they need air. Most of the time, they are almost invisible in the dark, murky waters where they swim.

A Breath of Fresh Air

No dolphin, marine or freshwater, can breathe underwater. They must come to the surface and take in air. A dolphin's nose, called a blowhole, is located on top of its head. The blowhole closes when the dolphin is underwater, so water does not enter its lungs.

This river dolphin swims through the dark water of the Amazon River in Brazil.

The Pacaya River, where two kinds of river dolphins live, is known as a black-water river. The water is the color of Coca-Cola due to chemicals released by forest plants as they decay. The Pacaya River merges with the Alfaro River, which is the color of hot cocoa.

Because river dolphins live in such dark waters, they do not rely on their eyesight to find food. As a result, their vision has deteriorated over time. Perhaps, because these dolphins have such poor eyesight, some South American Indians refuse to use dolphin oil as fuel for their lamps—they fear it will cause blindness.

Like ocean dolphins, river dolphins **echolocate**. They make whistling, clicking, and chirping sounds and use the returning echoes to understand the world around them and navigate. Echolocation is similar to the sonar system that

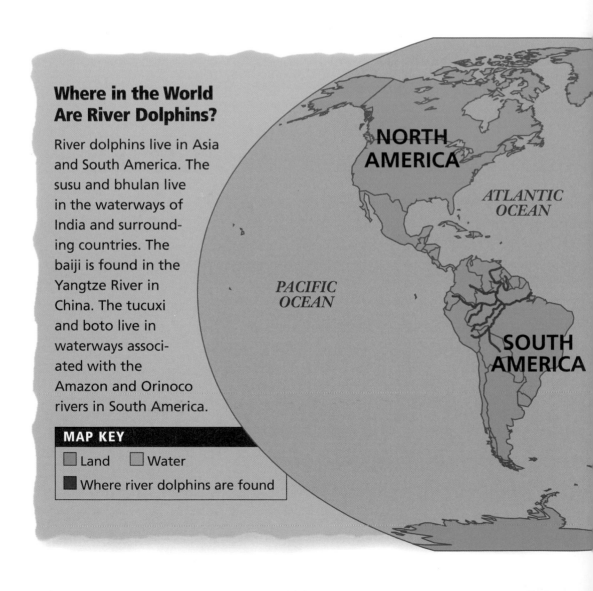

Where in the World Are River Dolphins?

River dolphins live in Asia and South America. The susu and bhulan live in the waterways of India and surrounding countries. The baiji is found in the Yangtze River in China. The tucuxi and boto live in waterways associated with the Amazon and Orinoco rivers in South America.

NORTH AMERICA

ATLANTIC OCEAN

PACIFIC OCEAN

SOUTH AMERICA

MAP KEY

☐ Land   ☐ Water

■ Where river dolphins are found

ships use to locate submarines and to avoid underwater obstacles. Each kind of dolphin sends out sounds at a different **frequency**.

The Susu and the Bhulan

The river dolphin that lives in the Ganges River is called the susu. It is also found in the Brahmaputra, Meghna, and Karnaphuli river systems in India, Nepal, Bangladesh, and

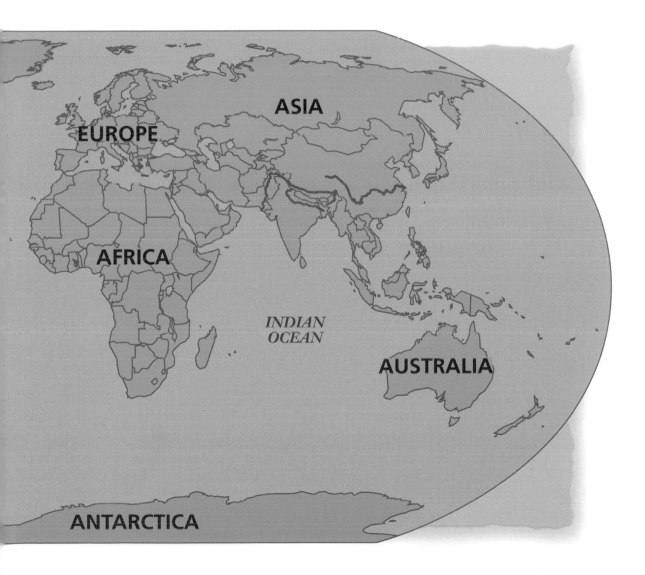

The susu can be found in the Ganges River. It has poor eyesight, so it must rely on echolocation.

Bhutan. The susu's skin is grayish-brown on its back and a bit paler on its belly. Some people think it looks like a crocodile because it has a long snout and its front teeth are visible even when its mouth is closed. The susu is 83 to 102 inches (211 to 259 cm) long and weighs up to 200 pounds (91 kg). The females are usually longer than the males because they have an extra-long snout.

The susu continues to grow for 20 years, and often lives more than 28 years. The females are ready to mate when they are about 10 years old and give birth about 10 months later, usually to one baby at a time. Young susus drink mother's milk for 8 to 9 months before learning to hunt for themselves.

The bhulan dolphin, which lives in the Indus River in Pakistan is very similar to the susu. It has the same coloring, and is about the same size. Both dolphins have very poor eyesight. Over time, the eyes of both river dolphins have lost their ability to form images, though they can distinguish between light and dark. With such poor sight, these dolphins rely on echolocation.

The Baiji

The baiji is very rare. Some people call it the Yangtze River dolphin because it lives in China's Yangtze River as well as in nearby lakes and small rivers that flow into the Yangtze. It is also known as the white fin dolphin.

The baiji has a pale blue-gray back and whitish areas on the belly. It is 5 to 8 feet (1.5 to 2.4 m) long and may weigh up to 265 pounds (120 kg). This dolphin has a long snout that is

The baiji is an endangered species that lives in Yangtze River in China. It can be recognized by its long snout.

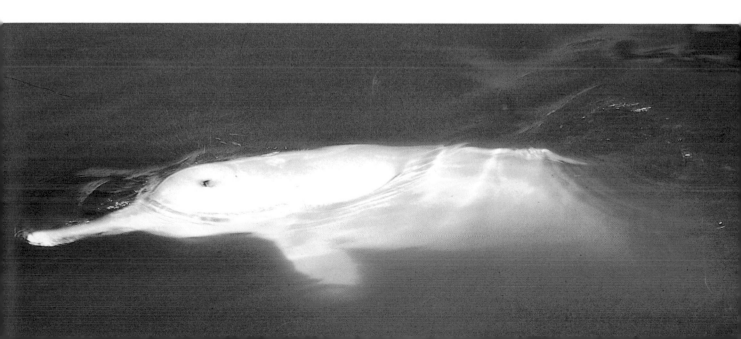

turned slightly upward. Although baijis often live in groups of about a dozen, they are also found in pairs.

The Tucuxi and the Boto

The tucuxi and the boto are found in the Amazon and Orinoco river systems in South America. The tucuxi is sometimes called the "gray dolphin," while the boto is known as the "pink dolphin." The names tucuxi and boto are Brazilian in origin. These dolphins see better than other river dolphins, but they still use echolocation to help them find food.

The tucuxi is small and agile. It often leaps through the air.

The tucuxi is the smallest type of river dolphin. It is 4 to 5 feet (1.2 to 1.5 m) long weighs 120 pounds (54 kg). It looks like the ocean dolphins you may have seen at a zoo or aquarium. It is shorter than other river dolphins and has a triangle-shaped fin on its back and a short snout. The tucuxi is the only river dolphin that sometimes leaps through the air. Groups of three to twelve tucuxis swim along the surface of rivers or lakes, leaving trails of spraying water.

Tucuxis often work together when they hunt. They corral schools of fish into a small area or drive fish toward a bank, and then enjoy a tasty meal. Scientists have discovered that tucuxis eat at least twenty-eight different kinds of fishes. Although they seem to prefer fish that are about 6 inches (15 cm) long, these dolphins sometimes eat fish more than twice that size.

Female tucuxis give birth about 10 months after mating. The baby dolphins are 27 to 31 inches (69 to 79 cm) long.

The boto, or pink dolphin, has a dark bluish-gray back and a pink belly. Scientists believe its rosy flush is caused by **capillaries** close to the skin. This river dolphin has a high-domed head and is about twice as long as the tucuxi. It measures 6.5 to 8 feet (2 to 2.4 m) in length and weighs between 175 and 340 pounds (79 and 154 kg). The shape of the boto's mouth and snout make it look as if the dolphin is smiling.

The boto uses its long, whisker-covered snout to search for food in plants along riverbanks or on the muddy riverbed. Sometimes the boto even uses its snout to dig in the mud.

The Hunt and the Feast

Most dolphins, whales, and porpoises eat fish, shrimp, and other small animals.

Most botos live in the
Amazon River in
South America. The
shape of the mouth
and snout make
these dolphins look
as if they are always
smiling.

When it finds its prey, the dolphin snaps it up and chews it to bits. The boto has 100 teeth in its mouth, and eats 6 to 10 pounds (2.7 to 4.5 kg) of fish and other river creatures each day. Although botos usually hunt alone, small groups often form in areas where two or more rivers come together.

The boto's large flippers make it an excellent swimmer. It can steer clear of tree roots and fallen trunks, make tight turns, or cruise slowly along the riverbed. When a river overflows, botos often venture deep into the flooded forested areas. When the floodwater begins to dry up, the dolphins return to the main river channels.

Swimming Upside-down

Botos sometimes swim upside-down when they are searching for food.

This mother manatee (left) and her two calves live in the Crystal River in Florida.

Chapter Four

The Manatees

If you visit a sinkhole or spring in Florida, you might see a manatee. This freshwater giant, which is also called a "sea cow," weighs more than 1,500 pounds (680 kg). Although all manatees are similar, most of the information in this chapter comes from research done on manatees that live in the rivers and along the coast of Florida. The Florida manatees have been studied more extensively than any other type of mantee.

At one time, these Amazonian manatees lived in the freshwater rivers of Brazil. Now they are being studied at the National Institute for Amazon Research.

Manatees and their close relatives, the dugongs, spend their whole lives in the water. Like dolphins and whales, their forelimbs have developed into flippers, and they have no hindlegs. Scientists believe manatees and elephants evolved from the same ancient grass-eating land animal.

There are three kinds of manatees: the Caribbean manatee, the African manatee, and the Amazonian manatee.

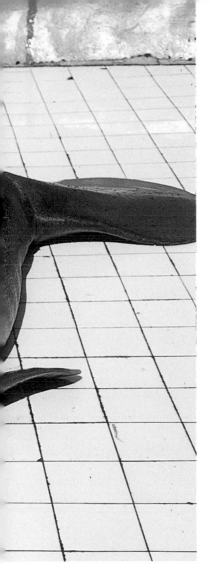

Caribbean manatees are found throughout the Caribbean Sea as well as in the rivers and along the coasts of Florida and Texas, Mexico, and northeastern South America. These manatees move back and forth between freshwater and saltwater environments.

African manatees live in rivers and along the coasts of several West African countries. They can be found as far north as Senegal and as far south as Angola. Like Caribbean manatees, African manatees divide their time between freshwater and saltwater.

Only the Amazonian manatee spends its entire life in freshwater. This manatee, found in the rivers of Brazil, Colombia, Peru, and Ecuador, is smaller than manatees in other parts of the world. It is about 9 feet (2.7 m) long and weighs a little more than 1,000 pounds (454 kg).

The Manatee's Body

Manatees are strange-looking animals. Their huge bodies have a thick layer of wrinkled gray skin covered with big, stiff hairs spaced about 1 inch (2.5 cm) apart. These hairs help manatees sense water currents. Manatees also have sensitive whiskers and bristles near their mouth. These help the animals find food at night or in muddy waters.

Below the skin, manatees have a layer of fat that helps keep them warm. Without it, they would have trouble maintaining their body temperature at 97.5°F (36.4°C). The stored fat also provides energy in the winter, when food may be hard to find. All manatees can live off their fat reserves for several weeks, and some can survive without eating for 6 months.

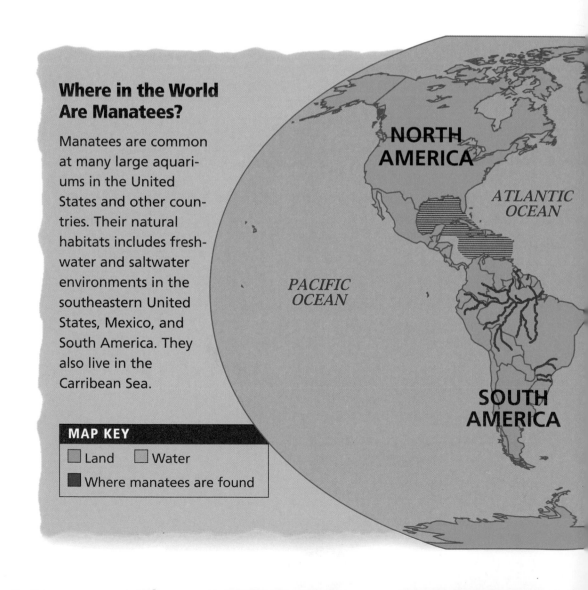

Where in the World Are Manatees?

Manatees are common at many large aquariums in the United States and other countries. Their natural habitats includes freshwater and saltwater environments in the southeastern United States, Mexico, and South America. They also live in the Carribean Sea.

MAP KEY

☐ Land   ☐ Water

■ Where manatees are found

NORTH AMERICA

ATLANTIC OCEAN

PACIFIC OCEAN

SOUTH AMERICA

Normally, an animal with so much fat would float on the water's surface, but manatees have heavy, solid bones that help them sink to the bottom. Manatees live in shallow water and move from one watery meadow to another. They do not eat seaweed or kelp. Instead, they prefer grasses that grow no more than 15 feet (4.6 m) below the surface. The digestive and respiratory systems of manatees are separate, so they can swallow food without getting water into their breathing passages.

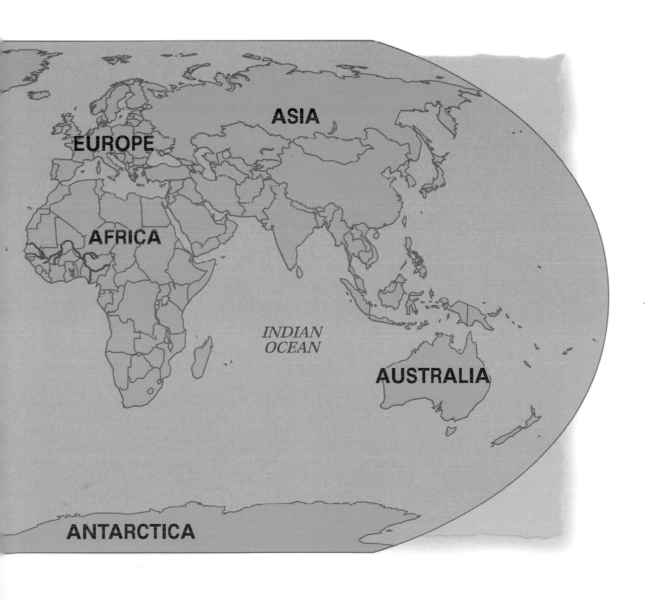

This huge manatee uses its peglike teeth to feed on a plant called Hydrilla.

Manatees have peglike teeth. Their big front molars are connected to one another and to the back of the jaw by **ligaments**. When the front molars wear down, they fall out and other molars move forward to take their place.

A manatee's eyes can focus clearly underwater. Glands close to each eye produce an oil that protects them from the salt in ocean waters. Although they have eyelids, manatees can also close their eyes by tightening nearby muscles. Behind each eye is an opening about the size of a pencil point. These tiny holes are the manatee's ears. Manatees have excellent hearing. And, although a manatee has no vocal cords, it can make sounds. Each manatee's voice is unique. A cow and its calf can identify each other by their voices, and certain sounds seem to have special meanings.

When manatees are above the surface of the water, they use their nose to smell the world around them, but when they are underwater, they close up their nostrils. Manatees use a special sense called "smell-taste" when they are below the water's surface. They leave messages for one another by rubbing their scent glands against a sunken rock or log. To read the message, other manatees move their snouts across the object and sniff.

A manatee cannot turn its head because the bones in its spine—called **vertebrae**—are so close together. All other mammals, including whales, have

A young manatee swims in the Crystal River in Florida. Manatees close their nostrils when swimming underwater.

41

seven bones in the part of their spinal column that makes up the neck. But manatees have only six.

A Manatee's Life

Manatees live alone or in small family groups called **troops**. They are gentle creatures, and can be approached by swimmers. When they feel threatened, manatees sink to the bottom and may stay there for up to 30 minutes. Normally, they surface for air every 10 to 15 minutes.

A mother manatee nurses her two calves. Soon the calves will begin to eat plants.

Females mate when they are 7 to 9 years old, and the calves are born 13 months later. Mother manatees give birth to either one or two calves at a time.

Newborn manatee calves can see, hear, and make sounds as well as adults. They are slate-gray—darker than adults—and weigh about 80 pounds (36 kg). From the moment of birth, manatees are good swimmers. A calf uses its tail and its paddle-shaped flippers to swim to the surface for air. A calf must rise for air much more frequently than its parents. A newborn breathes once every 20 seconds.

A young manatee drinks mother's milk when it is born, but soon begins to eat plants. It stays with its mother for about 2 years.

The Birth of a Manatee

A female manatee is about to give birth. As she slowly swims in circles, the manatee makes a series of high-pitched sounds. Every 4 minutes she pokes her nostrils above the water and takes a few quick breaths. Moments later, the baby squeezes out of the birth canal. It's a girl!

This warning buoy announces that a section of the river is closed to motorboats. Boats pose a hazard to manatees and other freshwater giants.

MANATEE

CLOSED

AREA

NOV 15 - MAR 31

50CFR17.108

Chapter Five

Giant-sized Danger

Unlike smaller animals, freshwater giants have few predators, but that doesn't mean they always live to a ripe old age. Their greatest enemies—humans—have put the hippopotamus, the river dolphin, and the manatee in danger of **extinction**.

The Hippopotamus

With an estimated world population of 157,000, the hippopotamus is not in immediate danger of extinction, so it is not considered an endangered species. However, the International Union for the

Hippos are not currently considered endangered species, but they may be soon if their grazing lands continue to be destroyed.

Conservation of Nature points out that the hippo is losing more and more of its grazing land every day.

Habitat destruction is not the only way that humans are endangering the hippo. In 1978, war broke out between the African nations of Tanzania and Uganda. Tanzanian troops hoped to overthrow the leader of Uganda. The wildlife parks soon became battlefields, and the soldiers shot hundreds of elephants, antelope, and hippos for meat and money.

Many hippos were killed, cut into pieces, thrown onto trucks, and hauled to market. Biologists who were studying the animals in Queen Elizabeth National Park in Uganda estimated that only 2,500 hippos survived out of the 12,000 that lived there before the war. The hippo population is growing again, but has not yet reached its pre-war numbers.

African tribesmen who live along the rivers inhabited by hippos use spears and harpoons to hunt these giant animals for their meat and skin. Hunters also remove hippo tusks and sell them.

In 1989, a ban was placed on the trade of elephant ivory. While this ban has helped the elephant, it is hurting hippos. Five times more hippo tusks were exported from African nations in 1991 than in 1988. A study conducted in eastern Zaire in 1994 revealed that the population of hippos had dropped by 50 percent since 1989.

African hunters sometimes kill hippos and sell their tusks. This has become more common since a ban was placed on the trade of elephant tusk ivory.

River Dolphins

Each year, enormous amounts of water are dammed to control flooding and to create hydroelectric power. Additional water is diverted to irrigate crops. As the human population grows, the rivers where dolphins live are fished more and more heavily. This means there are fewer fish for the river dolphins to eat. In addition, harbor developments, boat traffic, and pollution have contaminated many of the rivers where these animals once thrived. As a result, all river dolphins are endangered.

The baijis in the Yangtze River are in the most immediate danger. Although the Chinese government is planning to set up protected areas along the Yangtze, it may be too late to save the 100 to 300 baijis that remain. It is illegal to deliberately kill a baiji, but many are killed accidentally each year by people fishing and people in motorboats. Many other baijis die when lakes are drained to provide more land for farming.

The bhulan, which lives in the Indus River, is also scarce. Scientists estimate that only about 600 are still alive.

The tucuxi and the boto of South America are also endangered. They are hunted for their meat and oil and can become tangled in fishnets and drown. When these dolphins travel along the surface, they are sometimes killed by boats.

The Pacaya-Samiria National Reserve in Peru, a sanctuary for tucuxis and botos, is about the size of the state of New Jersey. It is run by the Peruvian Foundation for the Conservation of Nature with help from The Nature

Conservancy and the United States Agency for International Development. Within the reserve, fishing and hunting is allowed on a limited basis.

Although rivers and lakes make up only 1 percent of the reserve's territory, only 13 percent of the land remains unflooded all year long. During the rainy season, botos move

Some river dolphins are hunted for their meat and oil. Others die accidentally when hit by boats or when they become entangled in nets and drown.

onto the floodplain to feed on the rich vegetation that is then underwater.

Manatees

The manatee has been on the endangered species list since 1973. Although thousands of manatees once lived in the shallow coastal waters of the southeastern United States, scientists estimate that only about 1,400 manatees now live along the coast of Florida.

One-third of all manatee deaths are the result of accidents with boats and barges. Other manatees die because the seagrass beds they feed on are destroyed or polluted by dumping

Many manatees are injured or killed by boats. Here you can see propeller cuts on a manatee's skin.

and dredging. In addition, manatees living in the rivers and along the coasts of Central and South America are sometimes hunted and eaten by people.

In 1983, the Nature Conservancy established Crystal River Wildlife Refuge in Florida to protect and preserve wildlife. It is a refuge for manatees, fish, turtles, ocean dolphins, birds, and otters.

Into the Future

Despite all these efforts, the fate of the world's freshwater giants is questionable. Will the destruction and pollution of their habitats continue? Will people go on hunting these creatures? Without our help, the hippopotamus, the river dolphin, and the manatee may soon die out. The future of these special creatures depends on human beings. We have the power to destroy them or save them. It is up to us.

Glossary

bellow—a loud roar.

capillary—one of the tiny blood vessels between arteries and veins. They carry oxygen and nutrients to most body tissues.

dehydrate—to dry out or remove water.

echolocation—the ability to send out sounds and interpret the echo that comes back to gain information about the environment.

erode—to wash away. Rain often erodes exposed soil.

evolve—to gradually change over time in order to adapt to a particular environment.

extinction—the process by which all members of a group of animals die.

frequency—the number of times that something occurs within a given period. The frequency of a sound wave affects its pitch.

gland—a cell or group of cells in the skin that produces a liquid substance.

ligament—a tough band of tissue that connects two bones or holds an organ in place.

mammal—an animal that has a backbone, feeds its young with mother's milk, and regulates its internal body temperature.

nutrient—a substance that nourishes.

paleontologist—a scientists who studies fossils.

predator—an animal that catches and feeds on other animals.

school—a large group of fish or some other water creatures that live and feed together.

territory—the area in which an animal hunts, breeds, and sleeps.

troop—a group of animals that live together.

vertebra (plural **vertebrae**)—one of the bony segments that makes up the spine (backbone) of many animals.

warm-blooded—an animal whose body temperature remains about the same, regardless of its environment.

To Find Out More

Books

Darling, Kathy. *Manatee on Location*. New York: Lothrop, Lee & Shepard Books, 1991.

Horton, Casey. *Endangered! Dolphins*. New York: Marshall Cavendish, 1996.

Kaiya, Zhou and Zhang Xingduan. *Baiji: The Yangtze River Dolphin and Other Endangered Animals of China*. Washington, DC: The Stonewall Press, 1991.

Kendall, Sarita. *Ransom for a River Dolphin*. Minneapolis, MN: Lerner, 1993.

Reynolds, John E. and Daniel K. Odell. *Manatees and Dugongs*. New York: Facts on File, 1991.

Videos

The Magnificent Whales. Smithsonian Books and Marine Mammal Fund. Smithsonian Institution, 1988.

The Rescuers. Marina del Rey, CA: Bennett Marine Video, 1989.

Whalesong: Whales & Dolphins of the Pacific. Earthtrust Productions. Honolulu, HI: Distributed by Video Releasing Co., 1989.

Where Have All the Dolphins Gone? Marine Mammal Fund: The American Society for the Prevention of Cruelty to Animals. Oakland, CA: Distributed by the Video Project, 1990.

Organizations and Online Sites

Cousteau Society
870 Greenbrier Circle, Suite 402
Chesapeake, VA 23320
http://www.cousteau.org/AN/news.html

The goal of this group is to explore, understand, monitor, defend, and communicate about the Water Planet.

Dolphin Research Center
P.O. Box 522875
Marathon Shores, FL 33052
http://www.fla-keys.com/marathon/parks/dolphin.htm
This educational and research facility sustains a pod of dolphins in a natural marine environment.

Greenpeace USA
1436 U Street NW
Washington, DC 20009
http://www.greenpeaceusa.org
The members of this group are actively working to preserve the global environment.

National Wildlife Federation
8925 Leesburg Pike
Vienna, VA 22184
http://www.nwf.org
The group works to promote education, and to inspire and assist people to conserve natural resources.

Save the Manatee Club
500 North Maitland Avenue, Suite 210
Maitland, FL 32751
http://www.safari.net/~royal/manatee.htm
This club promotes public awareness and education of the endangered manatee.

U.S. Fish and Wildlife Service
Endangered Species and Habitat Conservation
400 Arlington Square
18th and C Streets NW
Washington, DC 20240
http://www.fws.gov/~r9endspp.html
This group works to protect endangered and threatened species, and restore them to a secure status in the wild.

World Wildlife Fund
1250 24th Street NW
Washington, DC 20037
http://www.wwf.org
This organization is dedicated to protecting endangered spaces and species, and responding to global threats to wildlife and habitats.

Places to Visit

Pittsburgh Zoo
Pittsburgh, PA
http://zoo.pgh.pa.us/wildlife.html
This zoo has birds, reptiles, fish, mammals, amphibians, plants, and invertebrates. The mammal section contains information and photos of the Amazon dolphin.

Woodland Park Zoo

Seattle, WA

http://www.zoo.org/home.stm

At this conservation and education institution, the exhibits focus on the value, beauty, and interdependence of all living things.

A Note
on Sources

In doing research, I think it is important to call upon as many sources as possible. First, I consult with a reference librarian who knows the collection well. Then I read books already written for young people on my topic. Next, I read standard reference works, such as *Whales, Dolphins, and Porpoises* edited by Kim Anderson and *Remarkable Animals: A Unique Encyclopedia of Wildlife Wonders* edited by Ulla Sunden, for general information. I narrow the search by consulting more specialized books such as Stephen Fry's *The Hippopotamus*, and seek out firsthand accounts such as Zhou Kaiya's *Baiji: The Yangtze River Dolphin and Other Endangered Animals of China*.

When possible, I make firsthand observations by visiting the animals in the wild or at zoos. I also speak with people who have seen the animals up close. For this book, I spoke with nature author Ann Nagda who traveled down the Amazon River to photograph river dolphins. I'm always on the lookout for newspaper and magazine articles related to my topic. For this book, I came across an article on pink dolphins in *Pacific Discovery* and an article on hippos in *Smithsonian*. I also watch videos, such as *Hippos: Killing the Land, Feeding the Lakes* and *Saving the Manatee*, which are both part of the World of Nature series.

—*Phyllis J. Perry*

Index

Numbers in *italics* indicate illustrations.

About the Author

Phyllis J. Perry has worked as an elementary-school teacher and principal and has written three dozen books for teachers and young people. Her most recent books for Franklin Watts include *Bats: The Amazing Upside-Downers*, *Hide and Seek: Creatures in Camouflage*, *Armor to Venom: Animal Defenses*, *The Crocodilians: Reminders of the Age of Dinosaurs*, *The Snow Cats*, and *Crafty Canines: Coyotes, Foxes, and Wolves*. She did her undergraduate work at the University of California, Berkeley, and received her doctorate in Curriculum and Instruction from the University of Colorado. Dr. Perry lives with her husband, David, in Boulder, Colorado. Dr. Perry's interest in hippos started a long time ago when she used to visit a hippo named Puddles in the San Francisco Zoo.